Another Husband Sissy Story

By:

Mistress Jessica

Introduction

Well where do you start, I mean I never started out with evil intentions in mind, though I have to admit that was exactly where I ended up. My name is Sally and I am a Dominant Wife, I know a few people would consider me an abusive wife, and I am fine with that except the only difference is that my husband actually enjoys me abusing him. It wasn't always like that, when I married Bob we were the typical married couple, we went on vacations together and built our nest egg together and all that normal stuff. We were married for about ten years before things started to change, and I never once thought that I would be in the position I am in today. Let us just say that I wear the pants in the family now, and there is no way I am going to give up that power or control, it became like a drug for me, I never realized just how enjoyable it would be to be the power in the house, but when I finally realized it I was addicted to it and I threw that power around with a heavy hand. The simple fact that my husband submitted to me just made me even more power hungry, it was like I could do no wrong, no matter how much I pushed the boundaries of the new relationship that was developing between my husband and myself I always found him to be accepting of my authority. In fact the more my husband capitulated to my wants, desires, and demands just made me want to do more and more. I don't want to get to far ahead of myself because that will simply ruin the story for you, and we don't want to do that now do we.

I guess I should start at the beginning though.

The Beginning

It was just another day; nothing special was going on, I think it was a Tuesday afternoon. I was lounging around the house trying to work up the courage to take on the laundry that had been piling up in the bedroom. It was a hot day out and I was relaxing with a cool drink, I think I was drinking a Mojito on the porch. The sun was shining and the birds were chirping in the trees of our backyard, I could hear the neighbor's lawn mower going so my relaxation was quickly interrupted which kind of put me in a touch frame of mind. I finished up my drink and left the porch to get the house chores done for the day.

As I entered the bedroom and began picking up the dirty clothes that had been strewn throughout the room as they often were during the week something caught my eye and I had to stop what I was doing as I pondered what lay before my eyes. It was tucked under the bed so I couldn't exactly make out what it was at first, in fact I had to get on my hands and knees and reach under the bed to get it. As I unfolded the article of clothing, I realized they were my white lace and satin panties that I had worn on our wedding day so long ago. I was rather perplexed as to why they were under the bed, in fact why they were under Bob's side of the bed, when I hadn't worn them since our wedding day, I had put them up in a box in the attic with some other clothing that I hadn't worn in quite a while and had forgotten about them. I got back on my knees and took a closer look at what else was under Bob's side of the bed. I could see what appeared to be a shoe box of some sort and slid it out from underneath, as I opened the shoe box I never in my life could have believed what I was seeing, inside the shoe box was some stockings and a bra along with some dirty magazines. I dumped the contents on the bed and continued to look through them, I found some of my old clip on earrings and bracelets that I had thought I had lost, plus more of my panties. I knew Bob enjoyed masturbation; there were times when I wasn't up for sex with him and he would slink off to the bathroom and jerk himself off, it never really bothered me to much that he did that. As I picked up one of the dirty magazines the women in the photos all looked like cheap sluts, as I paged through the magazine I started to take a closer look and it was then that I realized that all the women had cocks, this made me look at what was written in the articles and I realized that this was a cross dressing magazine. I couldn't believe my bob was looking at this material, and he was probably jerking himself off to this material as well. I was hut as well as pissed off, then understanding truly sunk in as I fell back to my knees by the bed. My husband was not only jerking off while looking at cross dresser magazines, he was in fact wearing these articles of clothing as well, which meant my husband was a closet cross dresser. I mean it wasn't like he was dressing up and going out into the world but he was doing something with my old panties, bra's and stockings I was sure about that. I sat by the bed for a long time as I tried to figure out when he was doing it, I mean I was usually home most of the time, and when he came home from work we always spent the rest of the day together, I pondered that for quite a while longer as the day slipped into the afternoon and the shadows from the trees made their way across the backyard. I put everything back into the box even my wedding panties just like I had found them and slid the box back under the bed. Needless to say the laundry didn't get done that afternoon, and I had a few more Mojito's to think about what I had discovered about my husband.

Home from work

I head his car as he drove into the driveway, and I put the fourth mojito back on the table on the porch as I heard the front door open.

"Sally…. Where are you?" asked Bob.

"I am out on the porch" I replied, though it sounded a little slurry to my ears.

Bob stepped out on to the porch still dressed in his business clothes. I kept staring at his crotch thinking to myself, I wonder if he is wearing my panties right now.

"Are you okay honey?" he asked.

"I am fine, though I think I had too much to drink this afternoon" I said as I glanced at the empty glass on the table.

"How many did you have today honey?" asked Bob

I didn't really know what came over me but I just had to know and I reached out and grabbed at his crotch, which surprised the fuck out of him, but he didn't move away. I tried to feel through his clothing to see if he was wearing panties but I couldn't tell, the one thing that I could tell was that his cock was growing hard rapidly. I moved on like a woman out of control, the belt came undone and the zipper was pulled down and I watched as his hard cock jumped through his boxer shorts and his one eyed worm was staring me in the face. I didn't want to talk about what I was thinking and I certainly wasn't ready to confront him about what I found just yet, I had to know more about what I was up against and I needed to have a plan on what exactly I was going to do about it. To cover for my rather intrusive behavior I took his cock in my mouth and started to suck on his cock right there on the porch.

"Honey what about the neighbors?" he asked.

Removing his cock from my mouth and with the alcohol in my head, I had to think fast.

"They will have to wait for their turn" and I took his cock back into my mouth.

I used my tongue right under the head of his cock and it wasn't very long before I could hear him start to moan and I knew it would be over soon, and I was correct a few moments later I could feel his hot cum in my mouth. I swallowed it all like a good wife and cleaned his softening dick and put it back in his pants.

"I am going to go take a nap in the spare bedroom sweetheart, why don't you be a dear and finish up the laundry for me" I told him.

I didn't wait for a reply but simply got up and walked past him and back into the house, as I turned to go to the spare room I looked back and saw him still standing there, probably thinking what the fuck just happened. I closed the door behind me as I entered the spare room and laid down on the bed to think about everything.

I imagine that Bob recovered from his stupor and I could hear him gathering the clothes and the regular noises of him starting a load of wash.

I tried to take a nap but all I could think about was Bob wearing those things. I was not repulsed by it, in fact I was rather intrigued by it. I was not sure if it was the alcohol or the fact that I just sucked off a cock but I was feeling very horny, and my fingers found their way into my shorts and under my panties as I began to play with my clit. Usually when I fantasize it is about some young hot man with muscles and a ripped stomach you know the typical male model figure, but for some reason all I could keep thinking about was my husband Bob crawling into bed on top of me while wearing stockings, panties and a bra. My fingers worked vigorously as my husband in his feminine attire began to enter my pussy as felt the silkiness of his bra and my legs wrapped around him so they could feel the stockings on his legs. It didn't take me very long to have one of the best orgasms I have had in quite some time and I had to wonder was that because of the fantasy of me wanting to see my husband in his cross dressing attire.

I napped for most of the afternoon, and when I finally did make out of the spare room I was pleasantly surprised to see all the laundry done and Bob was putting the last of the clothes away, he was very particular placing the neatly folded clothes into the drawers and making sure that anything hung in the closet was neat and buttoned and he even put things together by color in the closet. I had never noticed that before, and I had to admit to myself but not out loud that he was actually better at the laundry then I was.

What to do next.

I spent the next week trying to formulate a plan, I also found myself masturbating more and more and always it involved Bob in some sort of feminine clothing sometimes his hair was long sometimes he had makeup on but it was always something that involved him being more feminine.

I was really at a loss on how I should handle this situation and finally I broke down and realized that I was going to need some help with this so I called my best friend Ann and we scheduled a lunch for later that week.

When I arrived at the restaurant Ann was already sitting at the table we always get and was drinking a glass of wine.

"Sally it is so glad to see you I am so glad we decided to do lunch it has been to long since we got together and just hang out and chat" Ann said.

"I know we have so much to catch up on don't we" I replied.

The waiter came and he took our order, and of course Ann tried to flirt with him, though I have to admit he was a very good looking hunk of man. When he came back again I saw Ann slip him a piece of paper that probably had her cell phone number on it. He smiled back at her and pocketed the paper and gave her a nod.

"So what has been going on in your life, because I know there is something you are not telling me" Ann said.

"Things are ok with me, you know standard suburban life" I told her.

"Now Sally I have known you a long time and I could tell just by the tone of your voice that something is up, so spill your guts to me, I am your best friend and it is my job to help you with anything" she said.

I wasn't really sure how I was going to broach the subject but figured it was time to give it a shot.

"Well…" I started.

"Come on out with it" Ann told me.

"It is about Bob" I started.

"Did you catch him cheating on your or something like that because I will chop his little dick off if that is the case" Ann blurted out.

I laughed a little to myself not knowing how Ann would take what came next.

"No its nothing like that at all" I told her.

"I found some things under Bob's side of the bed and I am not sure how I should process the information" I continued.

"You see inside this box I found some my panties and stockings and some magazines depicting men who crossdress" I finished.

Ann's face was that of stone as she took in what I had just told her.

"Bob is dressing up as a woman?" asked Ann.

"No Ann I don't think it is anything like that, I think he is wearing my panties and stockings and masturbating while wearing them" I told her.

"Wow I never took Bob for being the adventurous one" Ann said.

This caught me off guard, I never expected Ann to be so accepting of the whole thing

"The point is I don't know what I should do about it" I told her.

She looked at me and smiled and then the smile turned into a grin an evil grin at that. I should have given more thought into what I was doing before I allowed Ann to know what was going on in my house, but the cat was out of the bag.

"Sally we are friends and I want you to know there are things about me that you do not know about, that no one knows about, but I am going to let you in on a little secret." She said. She then leaned in over the table a little bit.

"A lot of men fantasize about this stuff, they see the panties and the stockings as being sexually exciting and a men love to feel a little naughty, you would be surprised how many men go through a phase like this. The thing you want to decide upon is whether or not you want to encourage it." She said. Now it was my turn to have the quizzical look on my face.

"What do you mean Ann, I am not sure I am following you" I told her.

Ann sat back and laughed a little bit.

"Stan and I have been married just as long as you and Bob have been married and I am not sure how you are going to take this but since you are my best friend I might as well let this secret out of the bag so to speak. I caught Stan wearing my panties about five years ago and rather then get pissed off about it I actually encouraged it." Ann said.

"You encouraged it why would you do something like that?" I asked her.

"It was at that moment in time when I found him wearing my panties that I knew I could take all of the power away from him and I could become the head of the household, it was like over throwing the government and becoming the new leader of the family" She continued.

"Not only did I encourage it I made it mandatory, I immediately threw all of Stan's regular underwear and made him go out and buy panties. The same with his socks, they were all replaced by stockings, pantyhose, and when he is allowed to wear socks at all he must wear trouser socks." Ann said.

"But why would you want to do that?" I asked her.

"Oh Sally you have so much to learn" Ann smiled.

"Once he realized that I was now the one in control, he ever increasingly became more submissive to me and I became what some refer to as a Dominant Wife, I am the one that makes all the decisions now, I control the money, if Stan wants something he has to ask my permission first. Have you ever seen me doing any household stuff like cleaning or laundry, nope Stan does all that stuff, he cooks dinner and massages my feet, he has basically become my slave and I don't know how I lived in this world before I changed him." Said Ann.

This was so much information but the more I thought about it when I always saw Stan as being an attentive husband it was really just him doing Ann's bidding just like a slave.

"You like your husband like this?" I asked.

"I continue to modify him as my wants and desires continue to change. Most recently I have taken his orgasms away from him and I have put him in chastity so he is not allowed to touch his poor excuse for a cock. Everyone in this town thinks of me as the adulterous one, and yes I sleep with whomever I want but that is something Stan has agreed to and it actually makes his little cock so hard when I come home and tell him all about my sexcapades while he services me orally upon my return from my adventures." Ann smiled.

"Wait a second you go out and fuck other men and come home and your husband licks your pussy after it just got fucked by some young stud?" I asked her.

"Oh yes and I make sure those young studs fill my pussy up with their hot cum so my submissive husband gets a little treat so he knows I am not making my adventures up. Before you ask yes he enjoys being dress up as a little slut while I let him lick another man's cum from my freshly fucked pussy."

"Wow this is quite a secret you have been hiding from me." I told her.

"Yes and I am sorry but it is one of those things you don't let out of the bag unless you are sure the other party is ok with it. The fact that you confided in me that Bob is experimenting with wearing women's under garments was the information I needed to come clean with you." Ann told me.

"Now the real question is what are you going to do with Bob?" Ann asked.

I had to think about that long and hard and when I didn't answer immediately Ann continued.

"You really only have a three choices. One you could confront him about it and force him to stop, but they never really do, they just take it deeper and further off the grid. You could ignore it, but then you will always will be wondering what he is doing, and the panties and stockings are really just a gateway drug to other things, eventually he will get bored and begin to try something else. Now my favorite one is that you can control it, you can take charge of the situation and put Bob in his place which should be under your thumb, it is usually what they want when they get to that stage, they need guidance and who better to guide them into the world of further womanhood then a dominant wife to show them the way to show them how to choose the appropriate sizes and styles all the while they will understand that they are going to slowly but surely not going to be able to satisfy your needs as they become more of a sissy girl and you will gain yourself a lot of freedom and a lot of power that you will be able to wield over them and they will gladly except any of your rules of obedience and even punishment for any infraction. There are times when I get home and Stan has himself in the position over our spanking bench because of something he did that he wasn't supposed to. Trust me when I tell you have beaten his ass until he couldn't sit down and had to sleep on his belly" Ann said.

The waiter came back and I watched as Ann reached out and caressed his cock through his pants.

"Come on Sally lets go back to my place for an afternoon drink, I have some stuff I want you to see, and I am sure Stan is done cleaning the house by now. He has such a cute maid outfit that I think you will like a lot" Said Ann.

We left the restaurant and drove back to Ann's House.

Ann's House

On the ride over I told Ann how I had masturbated thinking about Bob in stockings, and panties and how excited I was and it was the best orgasm I had, had in quite a long time, she just giggled and told me that I hadn't experienced anything yet, that she was pretty sure my little visit to her house would open her eyes to a whole new world that is out there.

As we walked up the walkway Ann explained how since Stan could work from home that she kept Stan feminized all the time, it was only when they went out in public did she let Stan dress in men's clothes and it was only the outside that was now manly he always had stockings and panties on.

Her front door opened as she walked up to it, though Stan was nowhere in sight.

We entered a spotless home, I mean you could eat off the floors in Ann's house. I just stood there and marveled at how she was able to keep such a neat home. As I turned to take in the whole house it was then that I saw Stan, he was wearing a black latex French maid outfit with fishnets and high heeled shoes the whole works. He kept his eyes low never making eye contact with Ann or myself as he took his wife's scarf and hung it up by the front door.

Ann saw me looking at Stan who really looked very pretty and in fact was very passible as a woman.

"Stan lift up your dress so Sally can get a good look at you" Ann told him.

Stan's hands immediately went to the sides of his maid's outfit and lifted it up so I could see his the tops of his thigh high fishnets and I could also tell right away that his whole body was completely smooth and hairless.

"Now pull your panties down so Sally could see your pitiful excuse for a cock" Ann told him.

I was about to object but Ann simply put her hand up to my objection.

Stan let go of the side of his outfit and simply pulled his panties down and his cock was surrounded by a plastic cage and his balls were also trapped in this device so they protruded out and were obviously under some sort of pressure from the contraption.

"I also like to keep his butt plugged so on those days where I feel like wielding my big plastic penis around I have somewhere to put it. It is such a stress reliever to bend your husband over after a bad day and give him a good fucking in the ass" She laughed.

She then took me to the basement and showed me all the different contraptions that she had such as the spanking bench, and the cross, and other assorted tables of torture and pleasure.

It had been about an hour since we arrived at her house and she was explaining some machine that she had acquired along the way when I heard the doorbell ring. Ann didn't even bat an eye as Stan slinked off to answer the door. When Stan came back he handed her the paper that she had given to the waiter earlier in the day explaining that there was a young man at the door.

We made our way back up to the main floor and sure enough it was the waiter from the restaurant.

Ann didn't waste any time and simply walked over and began to kiss this young man deeply and passionately, I actually felt a little uncomfortable for Stan who simply stood there and watched his wife make out with a total stranger.

"When was the last time you saw another man's cock Sally?" She asked.

I wasn't sure how to respond to that question.

"I can't remember to tell you the truth." I told her.

Ann simply undid the waiters pants and they fell to the floor, in the next instant his cock was out and in her hand as she stroked it and it became harder and harder until the eight inches of his cock were rock hard.

"Come over here Sally and touch it" she told me.

She had such a commanding voice and I wasn't sure why I did it but I did just that and wrapped my hands around this young stud's cock and began to stroke it.

"Sally I think it would be a good idea for you to stay and watch this." She told me.

"I don't know Ann it seems like a very private matter." I told her.

"Stan come over here and make sure this young man's cock doesn't go soft or I will beat your ass" she told him.

"Now Sally this man's cock is big and probably much bigger then Bob's cock, you are going to need to learn to enjoy yourself and bask in the glory of your soon to be new found power." She explained.

I listened to her as I watched Stan get on his knees and start to suck the young man's cock without hesitation.

"I don't know Ann this is all happening so fast" I told her.

She noticed me watching Stan suck the waiters cock.

"Oh you will have Bob on his knees soon enough and you can watch him suck your lovers cocks and he will even eagerly swallow their cum as well if you tell him to do so, but you have to work up to that Ann. Do you find it exciting watching a man suck another man off?" she asked.

"I have seen some gay porn and it never got me excited before, but there is something about seeing a man who is submissive and wearing feminine attire sucking a big cock that does kind of make my pussy tingle" I told her.

"Well that is good to hear why don't you stick around and watch this big cock fuck your best friend in front of her husband and then you can see my little sissy Stan lick up this big cocks load of cum that will be in my pussy in a short while" Ann said.

I decided that I would hang out and watch but I wasn't ready to participate and Ann was ok with that for now.

So I sat in the corner as Stan sat on the floor in front of me and we watched Ann get the living crap fucked out of her, in all sorts of positions and I was very impressed with her agility as well as the waiters stamina. Stan sat there expressionless as his wife was thoroughly ravished by this young stud. They fucked for about an hour and when the waiter finally did climax he filled Ann's pussy to overflowing with his hot load.

We continued to sit there in silence as they finished up and she thanked him and told him that she would call on him again when she needed a good fucking and he was very happy to oblige and Stan got up and lead the young man out of the house. Ann just laid there on the bed with her legs spread wide and her crotch was covered in the young man's cum. I had to admit she had a very pretty looking pussy not that I had ever thought about other women that way but she was definitely turning out to be a much different best friend that I had known yesterday. Stan came back in the room and approached his wife and with a nod from Ann, Stan crawled up on the bed and between her legs and began to lap up the other man's cum.

"Do you see the power that you can wield" as she pointed down at her husband who just swallowed a mouthful of cum and continued to lick the mess that was between his wife's legs.

I nodded and found that I had a smile on my face and it was then I realized how wet my panties were.

I walked around the bed until I was able to look up Stan's little mini skirt and I could see his cock was swollen from trying to get hard in his cage and it was bulging out around the edges. It was also the first time I saw his but plug up his ass, it looked pretty big from what I could see.

I thanked Ann for all that she had showed me and that I had to think about everything and how I should proceed but I definitely liked the third choice from earlier, and I think it was going to be a lot of fun changing Bob into Barbra.

We embraced and said our goodbyes for now but I knew I would have a lot of questions for Ann, and she told me that she would help me in whatever way she could.

We made an appointment to go shopping one day next week she knew of a place that I could get some good deals on some equipment I would need once I was ready for it.

Some more advice

I had to admit my afternoon over at Ann's house really got me thinking about what I was going to do with Bob. I wasn't sure I was as strong as Ann was in breaking Bob the way that she broke Stan, and though Stan looked like he was totally enjoying himself in his new position I didn't see Bob capitulating to my demands like Stan did for Ann's little whims. I needed to get some more advice, it was time to call my sister Jane.

I told her that I needed to talk to her about something rather important and she decided to come visit the next day while Bob was at work.

Jane arrived promptly and she ushered me right to a chair to find out what was going on.

"Is everything alright Sally, are you and Bob having problems, are you ready to divorce his ass" She asked.

"No its nothing like that at all Jane, we are doing fine, well sort of it is just that something came up or I should say I discovered something and I don't know what to do about it. I took Jane into the bedroom and pulled out the shoe box it was then I noticed a pair of the panties that were in there were missing, and I figured Bob was probably wearing them today which kind of pissed me off.

Needless to say Jane was totally freaked out by this.

"That bastard, how could he do this to you " Jane said.

"Now Jane I think you are misunderstanding the situation" I told her.

I continued on about how it kind of made me excited and then told her about Ann and all the things that went on when I was visiting with her the other day. Jane sat there and let me finish everything all the time comforting me for what she thought of as totally disgusting.

When I was all done filling her in on all the details she looked at me with very empathetic eyes.

"So what exactly do you want to do about all this" she asked?

"Well I don't want to confront him face to face about this stuff and I would really like to make him into a submissive little sissy slut, but the way Ann did it to Stan it was like breaking a horse and I don't think I could do that to Bob. I have to come at this way from another direction, it is just that I don't know how I should do that" I told her.

In a second she whipped out her cell phone and was on the phone with someone name Nancy, who I imagine was some sort of doctor of something. Jane wasn't in the house for more than a half an hour before we were out and about going to

Nancy's office.

We arrived at Nancy's office and we were ushered right in even though there were patients in the room, evidently Jane had some clout with this woman. Nancy introduced herself and certain pleasantries were observed and soon Nancy turned to me and asked me to explain the situation to her.

I proceeded to again explain the situation, this time it sounded different to me though, this time it was me telling a total stranger a doctor at that how I wanted to feminize my husband making him into a submissive sissy so I could take all of his power of his manhood away from him so that I would be in charge and he would be totally attentive to me and do whatever I told him.

"Did you want him to remain a man with male genitalia or did you want him to have those removed as well" she asked?

"I never realized that was an option, but I think I would rather him keep his cock and balls, for now at least" I told her.

She actually looked a little disappointed in my answer, which made me a little nervous.

She asked some more questions about this and that, mostly dealing with specific things like if I wanted him to think of himself as a woman, which I told her know I want him to know he is a sissy.

Then she wanted to know if I enjoyed causing him physical pain. I had to think about this, I mean I was pissed off and all but I wasn't sure if I wanted to hurt him.

"Sally there is duality in all things and part of an accepted training path for creatures man and animal a like is to use both pain and pleasure. Now pain can be caused by a number of things such as physical pain, like if you were to spank his ass with something say like a whip or a paddle, there are other forms of physical pain like cock and ball torture which for some may be to much." She said.

I immediately sat up in the chair wanting to hear more about this cock and ball torture.

"A man's balls can take quite a bit of torture from hot wax, to slapping and biting, and of course there is tying them up or stretching them, and then of course there is needle play but if you are not into blood that last one is not for you." She told me."

There is of course another form of pain and that is humiliation, now since he probably already likes wearing women's clothing that humiliation will have to come from different paths, such as pictures or video on the internet of him dressed like a woman, to publicly humiliating him say at the store so the sales people will know that the bra he is trying on is for him things like that. One of the best forms of humiliation that usually hit home the hardest is cuckolding him, where you go out and fuck other men either with him present or not, and you don't allow him to fuck you anymore or if you do it is very rare an only when you feel like it, in other words he gets no satisfaction and as such he will become so easily sexually excited you will only have to tease him a pinch to get him to do what you want for you in the hopes that he may find some release with your approval" she concluded.

"Yes but that still comes to the root of the problem and that is how to make this happen without having to beat him into submission" I asked her?

"Well my dear that is where I come in, one of the things we do here at this woman's clinic is behavioral modification, and though we fly a very straight edge in the public's eye we have been working behind the scenes to shall we say change the course of history by pushing women's power limits to higher and higher ground" Nancy said.

She then reached into her desk drawer and pulled out a bottle of pills and handed them to me.

There was no indication of what the pills were at all on the bottle and to tell you the truth I didn't think I really wanted to know either.

"What will these do" I asked?

"Well for starters they will relieve your husband of his testosterone and replace it with a high dose of estrogen, this will cause a number of changes to his body both physically and mentally. Physically it will cause him to lose interest in his male attributes and become more docile and accepting of other stimuli that you can give to him. Now there will be other things that will happen as well, his body will go through changes he may even grow a set of tits, you should be prepared for that, his butt will fill out and his hips will shrink in giving him more of a feminine shape. He will be very emotional during this time and he may even cry a lot, but that is just the start.

He may lose interest in sex all together, but that won't be for long, just until he gets used to new desires that will spring up not to long after that. He will want to please you more then anything, and he will be open for what ever you want to do, his desire to be punished will increase even though his ability to please you will also be increased it will never be enough for him and as such he will continue to think he is not worthy enough for you. For that reason and for that reason alone, it will be him that brings up that you should start having sex with other people so that you can be satisfied. If at this point you have him in female clothing for most of the time, he will start to think of himself as a girl, not a woman, because you are the only woman in the house for him. Just so you know if you start bringing men home to the house, he will have a strong desire to watch you get fucked by them, and more then likely and I have seen this in a number of cases he will begin to be fascinated by other men's cocks. I wouldn't be surprised if he starts craving them, especially if you let him clean you up afterwards, it always seems that once they get the taste of cum in there mouths they are hooked and forever crave the stuff.

I sat back in my chair and pondered all that the doctor said about what these simple little pills would do, or atleast start to do and wondered is this really how I wanted my man to be. Then I thought back t that day in the spare bedroom, seeing him in my mind all sexy in my underwear and stockings and how he looked so happy and it didn't take but a second after that to tell the doctor.

"I understand and I think that is just they way I want him, I mean what would be better then for your sissy husband to be on his knees sucking your lovers cock, getting it hard for you so your lover could please you with it" I told her.

Nancy smiled at her

"I believe you do understand what you are getting yourself into, I remember when I first tried these pills out on my husband, he tried to fight it, but he never had a chance from the beginning, he used to be a macho man, masculine and even a bully. He hit me one time, it was really a slap, but he never struck me again after he started the pills. Now he sits at home and waits for me, usually when I come home I find him somewhere in the house with his little skirt up in the air fucking himself in the ass with a large dildo. Sometimes I will have my male friends come by the house just so he can suck them off, if he eats anything for lunch it is usually a mouth full of cum. The neighbors use him quite regularly. They used to be his football watching buddies, but now they come over quite regularly to get there cocks sucked from my husband whom they refer to a Sissy Michele" Nancy said.

"Oh there is one other thing you will need to do with him, you will need to get him on some exercise program, he is going to lose a lot of his physique and he will need to be working those muscles so as his new shape comes in that it comes it nicely." She told me.

"Are you sure you want to do this to him Sis" said Jane.

When we left Nancy's office I had the bottle of pills in my purse and some pretty devious thoughts in my mind.

Jane and I said our goodbyes, I truly wanted to get home and give Bob the first pill to get this change I had in my mind started. He thought he was being a little slutty pervert right now but he didn't know what I had in store for him.

The First Pill

I had devised a simple plan by replacing his Vitamin C pills with these new ones, Nancy had told me they look exactly like them and sure enough they did, so down the toilet went his vitamin C pills and into the jar went his sex change pills as I liked to call them.

I didn't notice anything different the rest of the day after he took the first one.

Nancy had said it would take a little bit before I would start to see any changes with him.

The Second Pill

The next day Bob was still his masculine self, he spent most of

the day watching sports on the television, he even called his

friend up and they went out to play a round of golf.

Still didn't see any changes in him.

The Third Pill

The third day started out like any other day Bob was doing his normal stuff, he was working out in the garage, getting all hot and sweaty doing some manly thing.

I was starting to get depressed it didn't look like the pills were working at all.

Bob came in and went to take a shower, he stopped to give me a very gently but sensuous kiss telling me how much he loved me. He was in the shower a long time much longer then usual, I didn't really think much about other then that. Later that night we were sitting on the couch watching some movie about something, when I placed my hand on Bob's leg and I noticed his skin was so smooth, and when I looked down it was clear that he had shaved his legs. I scooted over close to him and ran my hand slowly up his chest and found not a trace of hair there either. I was feeling frisky now and when my hand went inside of his shorts, they found his crotch hairless as well, and to my bigger shock and surprise was that Bob was wearing panties. I didn't comment on it, though my crotch instantly got a little wetter knowing that Bob was

changing and was now sharing his desire more openly. My

hand wrapped around his hardening cock, figured I better get

some from him before those pills made his penis into a soft

little girl clit.

"I want your cock inside of me right now" I whispered in

Bob's ear.

I followed up that with.

"I like you in panties and I am going to keep you in panties

from now on."

Bob's cock got harder in my hands at that. I had his shorts off and his panties exposed with his hard cock sticking up from the waist band. I crawled upon his lap and slid his hard cock into my wet and waiting pussy. It felt so good to feel his cock inside of me as his hands came to rest on my waist and he thrust upwards further into me. Meanwhile I began to play with his nipples first I just ran my fingers up and down on them and they actually got hard at my administrations, it was a small step before I was pinching them digging my finger nails into them. He seemed to be loving it so much that right after I came myself it didn't take very long before he was shooting his load inside of me. I laid there in his arms knowing that I loved him so much and we were so happy with each other.

I rolled off of him sitting next to him with one of my legs drapped across his lap, I took his hand and placed it on my crotch, taking his finger I ran it across my clit and then slowly I inserted it into my cum filled pussy, when I pulled his finger out it was covered in his cum, I brought it to my mouth and sucked his cum off of my finger then I inserted it back into my pussy and when I pulled it out this time I brought his finger to his own mouth, and he looked at me and then I almost came again when he took his own cum covered finger into his mouth and sucked it clean.

So I was pretty sure when all was said and done the pills seemed to be doing something for him.

The Next Day

When I awoke Bob was in the kitchen making us breakfast, it
was so nice to see him standing in front of the sink washing
some vegetables for the omelets he was making us, and he
was only wearing a little apron and the pink panties he had on
last night. I came up behind him and ran my hands over his
silky butt.

"I want you to know how much I get excited to see you
wearing women's panties all the time" I told him.

"I don't know why but I am really enjoying it myself honey, in
fact I wanted to ask you something" He said.

"I am not sure how to ask you this but I was thinking this
morning when I got up, would it be ok with you if I only wore
panties, I know how excites you when I wear them and I am
very glad of that, but I just have this deep urge to wear them
all the time. What do you think about that?" He asked.

I didn't know what to think at first, it was like he was playing

right into my hand, but I couldn't let him think that was the

case.

"Well what about when you go to the gym or to the doctor, do

you want them to see you wearing panties" I asked him.

He almost pouted thinking that I was against his desire.

"I didn't think about those circumstances but even with the

chance that someone else would see me in them I don't care, I

have just such a craving to wear them all the time, it is like

they make me feel sexy underneath. Please honey let me do

this, it would make me so happy, I would do anything if you

let me do this." He begged.

Now I knew those pills were taking affect for him to be

begging me to allow him to wear panties full time.

"Well it is obvious that you are enjoying wearing them and you don't seem to care what other people will think of you if they were to see you wearing them, but I think if you are willing to do anything for me to let you wear panties full time, I think you should do something that I want you to as well." I told him.

"Anything honey anything at all" he continued to beg.

"I think in addition to you wearing panties full time you should also begin wearing stockings as well I mean it is only fair that you get the fullest experience you can. I think you would look so hot in stockings as well, and who knows maybe I will continue to add more things to your full time wardrobe are you willing to do this for me, are you willing to do and wear whatever I tell you to?" I asked him

He didn't even hesitate, he immediately got on his knees and thanked me for allowing him the privilege to wear women's under garments. I mean he agreed to everything that I would be in complete control of him, and he would do whatever I told him to do.

He finished up making us breakfast which we enjoyed out on the back porch, he continued to only be dressed in the apron and the panties.

"Bob that was a delicious breakfast you made for us, now I want you to clean up this mess and meet me in the garage with all of your socks and underwear and don't leave any behind else I will spank your ass for disobeying me."

I left the porch and slipped into something more comfortable, and went to await Bob in the garage. When he arrived he had a handful of underwear and socks in his arms. I simply lifted the lid to the garbage can and he tossed them in. I knew the garbage was going out tonight so he would not have the chance to change his mind, not that it seemed he wanted to anyway.

"From this day forward you will only wear stockings and panties, you will never wear any more men's underwear again, so when you are at the gym working out you will have to take the chance of someone seeing you getting changed, and when you go to the doctor he will see just what a little sissy you truly are." I then handed him a pair of stockings and told him to go get dressed that we had some shopping to do today.

The Store

We arrived at the store and I could tell that Bob was feeling a little self conscious since this was his first time out in stockings and he was probably thinking that everyone could see he was wearing them when in fact nobody seemed to be paying no one else any mind. We immediately made our way to the ladies section and I started to browse looking for just the right type of panties that I wanted to see Bob wearing forever. It didn't take long before one of the sales clerks came over to help, Bob seemed like he was ready to bolt, but she came up to me and asked if she could help.

"Yes I was looking for a pair of really nice boy shorts, preferably in hot pink or red something like that." I told her.

"What size are you looking for" she asked.

Without blinking an eye, I turned to Bob and asked him what size was his waist, then I turned to the sales clerk and asked if she could calculate the appropriate female size that would fit my husband.

Bob's face went beet red and the sales girl chuckled.

"You are buying panties for your husband?" she asked.

"Yes we have a new agreement that he will wear panties and stockings full time from now one, you see I am going to make him into a sissy" I told her.

Looking at Bob after that statement you would have thought he had turned into a ripe tomato from the amount of blushing he was doing.

"Wow you have obviously taken control of your relationship with your husband, I know a few guys who are into that, and I actually think it is really hot seeing a man in sexy lady things. I think they are over here" She told me.

Sure enough it was the best sales help I have had in a store in quite some time. I made sure Bob thanked the girl for helping to find him appropriate panties for his new position in the household.

The sales clerk helped pick out two weeks' worth of panties in all different shapes and colors, and then we moved on to the stockings and we picked up a number of thigh high stockings and some pantyhose and even a garter belt for some fancy ones that needed it to keep them up. That was not all though the girl then took us over to the cosmetic department and explained which hair removal cream worked the best and continued on to some other things like nail polish for his toes. I was so taken with the girl that I gave her one of my business cards and told her to contact me outside of work and that maybe we could have some fun with her and her friends. All the while Bob was stuck carrying all of his new clothing items. I had thought about getting him a bra for himself but I knew a better store for that I mean after all every girl should have a custom fit bra, and that meant going to a special store where they would take his measurements and all that, I couldn't wait, but I would save that for another day.

We made our way to the counter to pay for our items, the lady was rather pleasant trying to make conversation.

"Oh you have picked out some lovely items my dear, they will look so good on you I am sure" she told me.

I couldn't help myself I enjoyed so much humiliating Bob in front of the sales clerk that I couldn't resist doing it again.

"Oh those are not for me, they are for my husband, I am now the man of the house and he is going to understand what it is like to be the woman of the house from now on" I told her. Seeing the look on the cashiers face was well worth it, and Bob had nowhere to hide, and I think he was enjoying it from the bulge in his pants. Needless to say the cashier didn't ask anything else about the transaction but finished up quickly and we were on our way home again.

The Sock

When we got home Bob went to go fill up his drawers with his new underwear and socks, it was then that I had an idea, thinking that a man isn't that thorough about things, I went to the laundry room and sure enough found a pair of socks in the dirty laundry basket. I knew I had him now just where I wanted him to move him to the next phase of his training.

"Bob what is this" I asked him.

Holding up the pair of socks in my hand, Bob had nothing to say as he knew he forgot to check the laundry room.

"Get your ass out on the porch and when I get there I want you bent over the couch out there" I told him.

He slowly opened the door to the porch and I went to get his big black belt.

When I got out on the porch he was leaning over the couch with his pantied ass up in the air.

"Now I told you to get every pair but you didn't think to do a good job for your wife, so now you are going to be punished for it so you will remember to do what you are told in the future." I scolded him.

I waited a second admiring his pink covered ass and then I raised my hand and brought that belt down across his backside with a loud crack. Just the sound of the belt hitting his ass and seeing him jump was enough to get my own juices flowing. I raised the belt up and brought it down again with another loud crack, I continued with five more blows to his ass with the belt and then I heard our neighbor on the other side of the fence.

"What are you doing over there Sally sounds like you are whipping someone pretty hard" He said.

Our neighbor's name was Bill, he was a recently divorced hunk of a man, I had fantasized about him a number of times when Bob was traveling for business but never in my life thought of doing anything about it, but now things had changed.

"Hey Bill, yes I am whipping my husband's ass for not doing what he was told to do" I told him.

I could hear Bob whimpering a little from the beating he had so far.

"Good one Sally, I could almost believe that one, but you can't get me that easily." Bill said.

I brought the belt down again a few more times with that loud crack making my pussy wetter each time I heard it.

"Well Bill you can think what you like but that is what I am doing, Bob has decided he wants to wear panties and stockings and be a little sissy husband, so one day soon I may invite you over to give me a good fucking, do you think you would be up for something like that" I asked him.

I didn't want Bob to think I was ignoring him so I hit him with the belt a few more times.

"Well Sally if that is the case you can give me a call anytime and I will show you what a real cock looks and feels like" Bill said.

By the time I was finished with Bob I could feel my juices escaping from my own panties and running down the inside of my thighs. Bob however had juices flowing from the other end as I could hearing him crying from the whipping he just got. When I pulled his panties down he had red marks across both cheeks that were bright red and welts were already appearing on his bottom. Pulling up his panties I told him to go do the laundry and make sure everything was done before he could come back into my presence again that day. I watched him slink away to do what he was told to do. I however went right into the bedroom and pulled out one of my dildos from the drawer.

I removed my panties and licked the tip of the dildo to get it slick but that was unnecessary as I slowly worked the tip of the rubber cock into my opening. I wanted to take my time as I worked the cock into my pussy deeper thinking again of Bill our neighbor, feeling the cock moving in and out of me my fantasies took a slight change as I thought about Bob laying on the bed next to me while Bill fucked me, Bob was wearing his new panties and stockings, his toes were painted bright red and he held one of my legs in the air as Bill plunged his very large cock into me, all the while Bob was telling me what a beautiful woman I was and how I deserved to be pleasured by a real man. It didn't take very long before I was screaming from the powerful orgasm that shook me to the core of my very being.

The chores

Bob kept taking his pills and his demeanor continued to change, he was now accepting the responsibility of doing all of the house chores, the cleaning the mopping, the cooking, the washing, I no longer had to do any of that and I enjoyed it very much. My sister Jane came over and was simply amazed at the different person that Bob had become. Now Jane knew about Bob but Bob didn't know that Jane new, and we kept that up until we figured it was time to embarrass and humiliate Bob a little more. I wanted to show Jane how docile he had become. So we planned for Jane to catch Bob in his little girl things. Bob was scrubbing the floor in the kitchen and was on his knees and you could clearly see his panties sticking out from the waist band.

"So Bob nice set of pink panties you have on under your jeans, does Sally know that you are wearing panties" she asked him. Bob practically jumped up to a standing position. That was where I came in.

"Well it looks like the cat is out of the bag honey, why don't you show Jane what you are wearing these days since it is obvious that eventually everyone is going to know you might as well start with Jane here" I told him.

With that said Bob simply removed his jeans and there he was in the kitchen in his hot pink boy shorts, and his nude thigh highs. His cock was bulging like it always did now when I embarrassed and humiliated him in front of others.

"Well Bob I guess you are no longer the man I knew" said Jane.

"So what other tricks have your taught your little sissy husband" asked Jane.

"Bob get on your hands and knees and kiss Jane's feet" I told him.

Without hesitation Bob was on the floor kissing Janes barefeet. Jane took it up after that.

"Suck on my toes you little sissy bitch" Jane said.

Sure enough Bob began to suck on each toe making sure to lick all around them.

Then Jane did something that even caught me off guard, she dropped her pants and turned around and told Bob to kiss her asshole.

Bob looked up at me and I simply nodded my head and then I watched as Bob spread Jane's ass cheeks and began to kiss her asshole.

"Get your tongue in there you little bitch" Jane told him.

"I want to feel your tongue inside of my asshole" she continued.

Bob pressed his face into the crack of her ass and really began to probe her asshole with his tongue.

I knew he was doing it right because Jane began to moan as she rubbed her clit.

I simply stood there and watched my sister masturbate while my sissy husband licked her asshole in the kitchen.

When Jane finally came, she simply pulled her pants up and told me that I was doing a great job with him, and that I should start getting him ready for real men to come over and fuck me.

I explained about our neighbor Bill who had a very large cock, but I wasn't ready yet, that I wanted Bob to be able to suck cock before I brought over other men to the house to fuck me, it would be so much better for Bob if he was to get the men hard by sucking them before they fucked his wife I told my sister.

She agreed with me and Bob went back to work cleaning the kitchen.

As Jane was just about to step out of the kitchen she told me that I should start calling Bob, Barbara. I had to admit it had a nice ring to it, and told her I would wait till he was a little further along.

Bob's Dinner

A few weeks had now gone by and it was time to get a feeling
for what Bob was thinking about all of this. I had decided to
take Bob out to a nice restaurant, we arrived at around seven
o'clock and were seated in a very private table and ordered
some wine. "So Bob my dear tell me what you are thinking
about all the changes that I have implemented so far" I asked
him.

"Well honey I have been thinking about all of this since day
one, and I had to admit this was something that was one of
my darkest fantasies that I have had for quite a long time. I
wasn't really prepared for you to take things as quickly as you
have, but I have to admit that though I thought I would have
put up more resistance about some of the things but for some
reason I found myself so accepting of your total authority over
me that I sometimes didn't believe I was doing the things that
I was. I wasn't really prepared to take over all of the
household duties but I realize now just how much you did

around the house, and seeing your approval when I do a job correctly makes it so worthwhile, I guess before that was something that I didn't do enough for you when I got home from work and I am sorry about that."

It was like listening to a totally different person, but he continued.

"I have so many feelings that surface inside of me wanting to do a good job, but at the same time I want you to punish me at the same time. I never realized just how much I feel like I need to feel your power through being spanked or whipped or other punishments; it is like the new way for you to show me you love me."

Now that I found very strange because I could totally understand it, when I did punish him it was very much the feeling of love that I had towards him.

It was almost like he was reading my mind, or else I got everything right, I had to give Nancy a call and fill her in on all that had happened.

"One thing that caught me off guard" he continued. "Is how perverted I really was, I mean when you started to embarrass me and humiliate me in front of others, I couldn't believe how turned on I became, it was something that was indescribable, like when you give me a command to do something utterly perverted, take for example when I had to kiss your sisters asshole, I mean that was terribly gross but at the same time it was so erotic that I couldn't think of not doing it. It seems the more perverted it is the more I want to do it."

I couldn't believe what I was hearing he was fully mine now and I knew I could do anything I wanted to him. We hadn't had sex since this all began I didn't want him to think of himself as a man would when in that position so I just never asked for it, but I knew he was masturbating constantly I had caught him a few times and I knew I was going to have to put a stop to that.

The food arrived and we continued our meal.

"Well I am very glad that you have accepted my authority over you and I have to admit you have come along way since we started, but you still have a long way to go."

"The next thing I am going to take away from you is going to be your own pleasure, you see I know that you are still masturbating since I stopped letting you fuck me, I don't think a little sissy in your position should be allowed to do that.

"I bought you a present" I told him.

I took the box out of my purse and put it on the table, he picked it up with a such a loving look on his face, and he began to open the box.

What was inside was a chastity device, he looked confused as to what it was, but when I told him, you could see him become very nervous.

"Yes my little sissy I am going to lock you cock up so you can't touch it anymore unless I let you, and there is nothing you can do about it." I told him.

"Yes dear, if you want my cock locked up then I will lock it up for you." He told me.

The waiter just happened to check in on us while my husband was holding the device, and obviously he recognized what it was right away and he no longer spoke to my husband as he realized who was in charge of our relationship.

I picked this restaurant because it was very private each table had a waiter but no one else could see what was going on at the table. It was then that I turned to the waiter and asked him.

"I will give you a very good tip if you take your cock out of your pants and let my sissy husband suck on it." I asked him.

The waiter not being prepared for this occurrence was taken aback at first but then he unzipped his pants and pulled out his rather nice size cock.

"Bob if you truly want to make me happy you will take the waiters cock into your mouth and suck on it." I told him.

Bob placed the chastity device on the table and turned to face the waiter and though he was hesitant at first he took the waiters cock in his hand and slowly brought his face towards it and opened his mouth and placed the waiters cock in his mouth.

My fingers immediately found there way into my panties as I watched my husband suck cock for the first time. He was clumsy and he gagged once or twice but I knew he would learn quickly as that was going to be the only sex he was going to be getting moving forward after this. If he had put up any resistance I was prepared to go back to the life we had before all of this started, but seeing him with a cock in his mouth just made me want to move forward full speed.

Now Bob was not that good at sucking cock and the waiter

was very nervous but eventually Bob found some sort of

rhythm and I could see the waiter was enjoying it and when I

knew he was getting ready to cum I instructed the waiter to

cum on the pasta that was still on Bob's plate. The waiter

pulled his cock out of Bob's mouth and proceeded to shoot a

massive load of cum all over the pasta on Bob's plate. He

tucked his cock back in his pants and left the table.

"Well eat up Bob" I told him.

I continued to play with myself as I watched the waiters cum

drip off the pasta that Bob was putting in his mouth. Two

more mouthfuls of cum covered pasta and I was had to bite

my lip as the orgasm rolled over me.

On the way home I informed Bob that I was going to start

calling him Barbara and that we would be picking up some

new dresses and skirts for him to wear including a little

French maid outfit with fishnet stockings for him to wear

around the house. I told him that I would do his make up but

he would have to start learning that himself, I explained that it

was important since he would be going out with me on dates

once he was passable as a woman.

When we got home instead of going into our house we

knocked on Bill's door and boy was he glad to see me, he

didn't even pay attention to Bob.

"Now Bill, if you let Bob suck your cock I will let you fuck me

here in front of him." I said.

Bill didn't waste a second his pants were off and he simply

walked over and started to shove his cock in Bob's mouth, it

didn't take much sucking to get Bill hard.

I simply pushed everything off Bill's coffee table with a loud crash and laid down an opened my legs wide and inviting for Bill's large cock and it was a monster. Bob sat on the couch right next to us I told him to get undressed and Bill laughed a little seeing Bob dressed in panties and stockings and even more so when Bob showed how his cock was now caged. Bill wasn't at all interested in Bob though he slid that monster of a cock deep into my pussy which was already wet from watching Bob with the waiter. Bill was like a true bull he made me cum over and over again, doing me everyway I could think of, when he finally did cum I made sure he came inside of me because I had a special treat for Bob or I should say Barbara.

As Bill pulled his cock out of my pussy it was like uncorking a keg of beer his cum simply started flowing out of my pussy, I quickly pointed at Barbara and set get down there and clean me up. Barbara was quick about it, he spent a good ten minutes getting every drop of Bills cum from inside of me and all that drooled down between my legs. When it was all said and done I simply pointed at Bills cock and told him to suck it hard again. Bill was much obliged to fuck me again once Bob got him rock hard again. When Bill was done fucking me a second time Bob was there to clean up another load of cum.

Follow up

Well it's been two years now and Bob is gone and Barbara has officially taken his place full time, he doesn't even have men's outer clothing in the house anymore. I put him on a diet and the pills eventually gave him hips like a woman and his tits even grew a little bit more, though after the first year we took him to outside the United States and gave him a nice set of tits, he wasn't sure about that but he didn't have much of a choice. Bill and I now live together and Barbara is well our little sex slave, Bill didn't want to fuck Barbara but after he got her tits Bill was all about anal sex with Barbara, it took a little while before Barbara started enjoying it as much as Bill does, but now I catch Barbara in her room with dildo's up her ass all the time. She was locked up the whole time, that was until one day she came in to my room crying and she told me that the chastity device simply fell off, and when I looked at her cock I could believe how small it had gotten I guess that was just another side effect from those pills that Nancy gave me.

These days Ann likes to borrow Barbara and she has Stan and Barbara do all sorts of kinky crazy things to each other while she films the whole thing for the internet, evidently Barbara has quite a following and makes enough money from her videos with Stan and Ann to help out quite nicely keeping us all well taken care of.

Right now I have convinced Bill that we should find another nice young man and make a second sissy, I mean after all if we could live quite nicely on Barbara's earnings sucking cock and being fucked in the ass by well hung men, then we could live even nicer with a second sissy. It took a little convincing but now we are looking around for our next project. Bill thinks that he may have found someone we are going out tonight to meet with them and see if he is everything we want in our second sissy.

I am so glad that I made the decision to step out of our ordinary lives and into a world of kinky crazy sex, it was the best thing that I had ever done. I have even convinced Jane to try the pills on her husband and see where it takes her, last I heard from Jane she was introducing stap on play to her relationship and that her husband was able to orgasm just from being penetrated with a ten inch cock. She was so proud of him that day, and because he can do that she asked me to keep his chastity key since she said he won't need to be let out ever again.

So moral of the story is if you want a life of insane sexual antics filled with orgasm after orgasm then sometimes you just have to go for it.

Well I have to go now our prospective Sissy is waiting for our arrival, he was instructed to be shaved and dressed and locked to his bed before our arrival, we are going to have a lot of fun with this new one I am sure.

See you soon.

A Note From the Author

Well here it is the end of another project, I get mixed feelings when I come to the end of a project, I enjoy writing so much that I am sad to be at the end but at the same time I know that now others will get a chance to experience my wonderful lustful and sometimes sadistic thoughts via the story or the assignment. I just have so much fun writing about the experiences I have with my own submissive play things, they are such good little boi's all dressed so pretty and they do whatever I ask of them, well they know they will be punished if they don't.

So now it is your turn to once again do what I ask of you.

I would like to hear from you, I am going to give you my personal email address so you can contact me so that I can get your feedback on the stories and the assignments and anything else you would like to tell me about. I would love to hear about your own stories and experiences, I just love it when I get email from the people who read my work, so don't hesitate to contact me, who knows maybe I will give you a special assignment just for you.

Write to me soon.......

Love

Mistress Jessica

Mistressjessica01@gmail.com

www.ingramcontent.com/pod-product-compliance
Lightning Source LLC
Chambersburg PA
CBHW072338290526
45794CB00002B/930